Original title:
Tropical Tides

Copyright © 2025 Creative Arts Management OÜ
All rights reserved.

Author: Gabriel Kingsley
ISBN HARDBACK: 978-1-80586-334-2
ISBN PAPERBACK: 978-1-80586-806-4

Dunes that Hold the Memories

In sandy hats we strut and sway,
With crabs that grin in a cheeky way.
We tumble down like playful stones,
While gulls giggle in funny tones.

The sun rolls high, the lizards dance,
In flip-flops lost, we prance and prance.
Each grain a tale, each bead a jest,
In dunes that cradle our silly quest.

Glistening Waters of Forgotten Shores

Oh what a splash, oh what a dive,
Mermaids swear they saw a live.
With waves that crash in fits of glee,
We swim away from jellyfish's spree.

The beachball flies, we duck and weave,
In salty chaos, we believe.
With sunburned tales and sandy fries,
We wave our troubles as they fly.

Petals on the Wind, Whispering Stories

A flower's flurry, a whirlwind laugh,
Chasing petals, we take a gaff.
With bees in hats, we dance the beat,
In whispered tales, our giggles meet.

The breeze teases, it pulls and tugs,
We stumble over playful hugs.
Like joyful butterflies on scruffy trails,
We launch our dreams like paper sails.

Cascades of Cloud Shadows

Up above, the clouds they play,
A carousel in the sky's ballet.
We leap on shadows as they drift,
Trading our squabbles for a gift.

With rainclouds dressed in jester's gear,
They shower us with laughing cheer.
Oh, the puddles, our laughter's friend,
In silly dances that never end.

Where the Surf Meets the Sky

The seagulls squawk, they dance and dive,
While beach balls bounce, oh how they thrive!
Sandy toes are all the rage,
As flops and slips become the stage.

Umbrellas flip in random flight,
Sunburned noses, quite a sight!
Laughter rolls like waves on shore,
As sunscreen battles beachy war.

Crabs take along their weekly snacks,
While kids make castles, dodging cracks.
Friendships bloom like seaweed clumps,
With goofy faces and silly jumps.

Mirage of the Sunset Lagoon

The sunset gleams with colorful flair,
While ducks decide who gets to share.
Floaties drift like lazy dreams,
As sunlight dances, or so it seems.

A coconut fell—what a big bang!
The beachgoers laugh as the lifeguard sang.
In this paradise, hiccups are loud,
Where giggles float above the crowd.

Sky's painted pink with splashes of gold,
Stories of adventures eagerly told.
With flip-flops flying high in delight,
This lagoon's fun by day and night.

Secrets of the Island Flora

The flowers gossip, their petals sway,
Whispering secrets, come out to play.
Cacti wear hats, they think it's cool,
While vines talk smack, that's just their rule.

A pineapple wears a swimsuit bright,
While ferns throw shade, judging the light.
The palm trees sway, gossiping palms,
With coconuts giggling in leafy balms.

Butterflies flutter with flair and grace,
As bees buzz by, claiming their space.
In this garden, humor blooms wide,
Where every leaf has a fun little side.

Driftwood Memories in Dappled Sunlight

Driftwood logs tell tales of the sea,
Of crabs and fishes, just wait and see!
Pinecones act like driftwood too,
In this whimsical world, nothing's askew.

Sunlight dapples the sandy ground,
Where jokes of the tide are cheerfully found.
Every snapshot holds a laugh,
As memories drift along the path.

Shells wear hats like a tropical fan,
While seaweed wiggles, oh what a plan!
In these moments, joy is the theme,
As laughter ripples like a sweet dream.

A Symphony of Shorelines

Waves are dancing, what a sight,
Sandcastles wobbling, a toppling fright.
Crabs in tuxedos scuttle with glee,
As seagulls sing out their off-key spree.

Flip-flops forgotten, lost in the tide,
Sunburned noses, a source of pride.
Ice cream cones spill, oh what a mess,
As laughter echoes, we simply bless.

Shores of Forgotten Memories

Forgotten flip-flops, a mystery pair,
Lurking like secrets in salty air.
Old treasures buried, cringe-worthy finds,
Half-eaten sandwiches and jellyfish pines.

Umbrellas topple in the morning breeze,
Chasing after them like wayward keys.
Sunscreen battles, slip and slide,
Leaving us sticky, but full of pride.

The Laughter of Ocean Children

Barefoot adventures on golden grains,
Tickled by waves, ignoring the stains.
Frog-jumping games at the shoreline's bend,
Making new friends, to splash and pretend.

Seashells ring like bells on our toes,
While dolphins giggle in joyful rows.
Grown-ups complain about kids' wild schemes,
But we're all pirates chasing our dreams.

Emerald Depths and Golden Sands

In emerald waters, we splash and dive,
Building the best mermaid fort to thrive.
A treasure map drawn with a crayon stain,
Leading to snacks, but we'll never complain.

Sun hats askew, we picnic in style,
With sandwiches shaped like a goofy smile.
Seashells gossip about nearby fish,
Hatching plans for a grand summertime wish.

The Dance of Rain and Sunshine

Raindrops twirl like dancers bold,
They skip and slide on streets of gold.
Sunshine giggles, shines so bright,
Wants a turn to join the light.

Puddles splash with laughter loud,
While umbrellas form a crowd.
Raindrops plunge with joyful cheer,
Then vanish fast, not staying near.

Journey into the Heart of the Ocean

A fish in flip-flops takes a stroll,
While jellyfish dance, that's their role.
Starfish flip like they own the place,
Seahorses giggle, just in case.

Crabs are cooking with no recipe,
"Seaweed salad's just for me!"
Turtles wave with shells so bright,
As dolphins dive, oh what a sight!

Serenade of the Calypso

A parrot sings with notes so sweet,
While rum drinks tumble, what a treat!
Limes roll past like playing balls,
Palm trees sway to nature's calls.

The conch shell plays a goofy tune,
Each beat bursts forth like a balloon.
Under the sun, they dance with glee,
Echoes of laughter, wild and free.

Invitations from the Bahama Breeze

Cocktails clink in the warm night air,
A breeze whispers secrets, light as a hair.
Flip-flops shuffle on sand that's warm,
Giggling grains perform a charm.

Palm fronds wave as if to say,
"Let's dance until the break of day!"
The stars giggle, twinkling above,
While crickets sing of ocean love.

A Dance of Ocean Waves

The water does the cha-cha, oh so sly,
Froggy flips in style, waving bye-bye.
Seagulls join the party, with a squawk and dive,
Even the crabs are jiving, oh, how they thrive!

Sandcastles wave hello, then topple down,
Surfboards chase the waves with a goofy frown.
The sun's a spotlight, shining bright and bold,
As beachballs bounce around with laughter untold.

Snorkelers play hide and seek with fish galore,
While beach hats fly off as they dodge the shore.
It's a merry jaunt, where laughter never fades,
In this fun-filled dance, all worries evade.

Secrets Beneath the Palm Canopy

Beneath the palms, where monkeys swing and play,
Squirrels wear sunglasses, come join the fray.
A parrot spills secrets, with flair and strut,
While crabs plot mischief in their sandy hut.

The coconuts gossip, each round and sweet,
Whispering stories, oh, what a treat!
Lizards sunbathe like they own the scene,
While turtles ponder life, slow and serene.

In a hammock swung low, a sloth takes a nap,
Waking for snacks, then back to the flap.
Palm leaves giggle softly in the balmy breeze,
Nature's laugh is infectious, putting hearts at ease.

Sun-Kissed Shores and Driftwood Tales

On sun-kissed shores, the laughter lines grow,
As children write stories in the sand below.
Driftwood shivers, transformed into a chair,
Where crabs wear tiny hats, without a care.

Seashells sing softly, a clam-boogie tune,
While kids chase the waves beneath the bright moon.
The surf sculpts a mermaid with a wink and a smile,
As jellyfish dance, floating free for a mile.

Beach umbrellas flutter like kites in the sky,
As the waves go splash, oh my, oh my!
In a swirl of hues, every shade glows bright,
An ocean of giggles under the starry night.

The Gilded Horizon

The horizon blinks like a cheeky eye,
As sunsets descend, painting gold in the sky.
Fish put on a show, leaping up high,
While sunbathers giggle and let out a sigh.

Lost flip-flops wander, looking for their mate,
Each wave brings a wink, it's never too late.
Surfers glide gracefully, but one takes a fall,
Splashing in the sea, oh, it's a ball!

Whales hum a tune, serenading the light,
As dolphins throw parties, flipping in delight.
Laughter ripples softly along the bright shore,
Where every grain of sand holds fun, evermore.

Dance of the Hibiscus Blooms

Under sunlit skies they sway,
Hibiscus blooms in bright array.
They dance like clowns on a sunny day,
With petals drinking lemonade.

Bees buzz in a haphazard flight,
Trying to find their dance partner right.
But one gets dizzy, oh what a sight,
And tumbles down, but laughs with delight.

Their colors blaze, a joyful riot,
In breezy whispers, they start a riot.
Each flower flaunts, says, "Come and try it!"
As bees just chuckle, feeling the diet.

So if you stroll through paths so bright,
Join in the giggles, make it a night.
With hibiscus winks and laughter in sight,
You'll find yourself dancing, what pure delight!

Echoes beneath the Coconut Canopy

Beneath the palms, the coconuts grin,
Gossiping secrets of where they've been.
One says, "I rolled down and fell with a spin,"
And everyone chuckles, where to begin?

The monkeys swing with comic flair,
Dropping coconuts without a care.
A nearby parrot is quick to declare,
"That wasn't me, it was just the air!"

They mimic the waves, they mimic the breeze,
Sharing tales with the rustling leaves.
From goofy dances to silly wheeze,
The canopy's laughter brings giggles with ease.

So bask in the shade where stories unfold,
Where humor's as rich as the finest gold.
And if you listen, you'll feel the old,
Echoes of laughter, never controlled.

Waves that Kiss the Golden Sands

The waves come in with a tiptoe stroll,
Winking at shells, oh what a goal!
They tickle the toes, say, "How's your soul?"
Then run away like they've lost control.

A crab in a tux gets ready to dance,
But slips on the sand with a clumsy prance.
The seagulls laugh, they take a chance,
As waves just giggle, wild in their romance.

The sunset blushes, paints all around,
As waves bring laughter, a playful sound.
They rush to the beach, then scatter the ground,
In a game of tag, joyfully unbound.

So when you stand by the shimmering view,
Join in the fun, let laughter ensue.
With waves and sand, all warm and blue,
It's a playful party just waiting for you!

Lullaby of the Salt-Kissed Night

As night falls soft with a twinkle light,
Stars peek down, oh, what a sight!
The crickets chirp, saying goodnight,
While waves hum sweetly, hearts feeling bright.

A lobster in shades is ready to munch,
While fish throw a party, a glorious brunch.
They laugh and they dance, a sea creature bunch,
While the moon beams down, joining the punch.

The cool breeze whispers a playful tune,
As sea turtles dance beneath the moon.
With every splash, there's a silly swoon,
The ocean's lullaby, a playful croon.

So snuggle up tight, let the laughter flow,
As waves tell tales while putting on a show.
In salt-kissed dreams, let your worries go,
With the night's sweet humor, a charming glow.

Mosaic of Tropical Reflections

A parrot wearing shades, oh what a sight,
Sipping a drink, he thinks he's so bright.
The palm trees dance, but not in a line,
They sway to the music, feeling just fine.

Flip-flops are flapping, it's quite the display,
While sunbathers argue on who's having a spray.
A crab scuttles by with a flip and a toss,
Claiming the beach, like a boss, he's the gloss.

The sun sets low, it's a glittering tease,
A sea cucumber's lost in the gentle breeze.
With laughter and joy under skies so blue,
These silly beach moments, who needs a zoo?

A dolphin appears with a splash and a song,
He pokes fun at fish, surely something's wrong.
The waves giggle too, as they roll on the sand,
In this mosaic place, joy's always at hand.

Beneath the Canopy of Stars

Stars twinkle bright, like diamonds in flight,
While crickets debate who'll sing through the night.
A raccoon rolls in, a bandit with flair,
He joins the fiesta, spreading joy everywhere.

With coconuts falling, what a clumsy event,
One hits a fellow, now he's slightly bent.
The moon chuckles softly at the jester's fair dance,
While a sea turtle dreams of a sunken romance.

The sea breeze carries whispers, both silly and sweet,
Of mermaids who giggle while playing with feet.
A hammock swings low, oh what a delight,
As friends crack some jokes under stars shining bright.

Beneath this grand canopy, laughter resounds,
With every odd creature that leaps and rebounds.
The night may be quiet, but joy fills the air,
In this world of wonder, we find laughter to share.

Currents of Paradise and Passion

The waves are a dance floor, splashes galore,
While sunburned tourists all scream for more.
A backdrop of palm trees, each one with a grin,
They sway in the rhythm, inviting us in.

A seagull swoops down with a hot dog in tow,
As beachgoers wonder, "How did he know?"
With shouts and with giggles, we run and we play,
Chasing the tide like it's just another day.

Beneath a sunhat, an old man does nap,
Dreaming of fish that might fit in his lap.
Meanwhile, a toddler collects shells with glee,
Until a wave sweeps them — oh, woe is me!

The fun never halts, like a loop in a tune,
With sand sculptors carving a wacky cartoon.
In this playful paradise, each moment a blast,
We cherish the laughter that's sure to last.

Footprints in the Warm Evening Sand

Footprints zigzag like a drunken parade,
With dogs chasing tails, oh the chaos they made!
While kids build a castle with buckets and shovels,
Their laughter resounds, like sweet little bubbles.

A hermit crab darts, dressed up in his shell,
He struts like a king, oh how well he can dwell!
With ice cream in hand, a drizzle goes bam,
Turns into a sticky, sweet summer jam.

The sun dips low, painting the sea in gold,
While stories unfold, each one more bold.
A duck joins the party, with friends in a line,
Waddling around like it's some grand design.

As stars come out, the beach turns to dream,
With giggling waves that laugh and gleam.
In the evening glow, with joy we expand,
Leaving our marks, in the warm evening sand.

Whispers of the Ocean Breeze

The seagulls squawk in a clever way,
They tease the crabs who wish to play.
The beach ball bounces with silly cheer,
While sunburned tourists sip their beer.

The surfers ride on waves of joy,
Each wipeout feels like a cheeky ploy.
Flip-flops fly in a sandy dance,
As laughter echoes, given the chance.

A sunhat flies like a paper kite,
Chasing sunsets in fading light.
The jellyfish float with grace and glee,
But watch your toes; they sting, you see!

In every wave, a chuckle hides,
As we all surf on silly tides.
So join the fun, leave worries behind,
For life's a joke, let's unwind.

Sunlit Shores and Dreaming Palms

Under the palms, we play some games,
The squirrels here have quite the names.
Fred the Nut and Sal the Cat,
Join us all for a silly chat.

A lemonade stand wobbles and shakes,
With mischievous plans for pesky flakes.
We sip too fast, and what a surprise,
Now we're all just sticky and wide-eyed!

The sun makes shadows that wobble and sway,
A dance-off starts without delay.
Tanned legs twirling, hats flying high,
We laugh till we're puffed and sigh.

Seashells whisper the strangest tales,
Of dancing dolphins and flying snails.
So grab your friends, let's just be bold,
In this sunny land, fun never gets old.

Rhythm of the Coral Waves

The fish parade in flashy hues,
While crabs wear hats, it's quite the muse.
An octopus plays a saxophone,
As mermaids giggle, quite alone.

Coconuts roll like bowling balls,
Careful, they scratch; it's silly falls.
We race with tides and jump with glee,
While seaweed tickles each pizza tree.

The starfish holds a talent show,
With smooth moves that steal the flow.
But when they trip on their own two arms,
We laugh until we lose our charms.

So surf the curls of liquid fun,
Join in, everyone; we've just begun.
For in this whirl of splashes bright,
You'll find laughter and pure delight.

Serenade of Seafoam Secrets

In the mist, secrets waltz around,
As beachcombers search for lost treasure found.
A rogue wave crashes, takes hats away,
And giggles chase them through the bay.

Clams gossip with a sassy tone,
As dolphins make their happy moan.
Shells play tag with a salty breeze,
While sandcastles tumble like soft cheese.

The seafoam dances, twirls, and flips,
While flip-flops hide—look out for slips!
We build our dreams on grains so fine,
In this whimsical world, all things align.

So raise a toast to this salty spree,
For every wave brings more glee.
Laugh with the sea, its playful sway,
In this seafoam song, we'll forever play.

A Song of Whispering Winds

The breeze sings low, a tickle here,
A crab is dancing, my drink's unclear.
The seagulls squawk, they steal my fries,
As I chase sand, oh how time flies.

The sun's a joker, bright and bold,
Playing peek-a-boo, oh what a show!
Flip-flops flop as I try to run,
For fried fish jokes are just too fun!

A parrot squawks, 'You're looking fine!'
As I slip on sand, oh never mind!
My beach ball bounces and rolls away,
A game of tag, come what may!

Oh, laughter rings like waves in play,
Where time is lost in a sunny stay.
Every giggle adds to the ride,
In this world where fun won't hide.

Beneath the Veil of Coconut Trees

Coconuts drop with a soft thud,
While I snack on chips, covered in crud.
The palm fronds sway, in playful tease,
As I dance with shadows, caught in the breeze.

A monkey grins, perched high with flair,
Swiping my hat, I chase in despair.
Laughter erupts as I swirl in fight,
Underneath these leaves, a comical sight.

Sandcastles rise, but soon they'll fall,
Waves laugh loudly, they're having a ball.
I find a crab, who thinks he's king,
But lose my shoes, oh the joy they bring!

With each wave crash, life's absurd spins,
Out here with friends, everyone wins.
Jokes fly high like kites in the sky,
As we soak in fun, just you and I.

Fragments of a Dusk Horizon

The sun yawns wide, splashes of gold,
As I try to catch moments untold.
A flip-flop finds a way to escape,
While I trip on my towel, what a shape!

The sky's a canvas, painted with glee,
As dolphins splash drinks, just wait and see.
Sunset cocktails, oh what a mix,
Stirred by the tides, with a zany fix.

Pufferfish giggle with cheeks puffed out,
While I argue with seagulls, there's no doubt.
'Your fries are mine!' they cackle and flap,
As I plan my escape from this silly trap!

With every laugh, as day turns to night,
This sandy stage feels just right.
Memories glimmer like stars afar,
Living in whimsy, my favorite bazaar.

Radiant Life Within the Reef

Beneath the waves, where colors gleam,
Fish swirl around in a silly dream.
A clownfish waddles like he's on cue,
While I fumble with gear, so much to do!

Coral castles teem with surprise,
An octopus waving just caught my eyes.
My snorkel's leaking, bubbles in flight,
As I splash around with pure delight.

Starfish giggle, all clad in pink,
While I try to balance, I start to sink.
A turtle's grinning, taking a ride,
As I float along, losing my pride.

Under the sea, laughter's a feast,
Where every creature's a playful beast.
In the heart of the reef, joy never ends,
In this funny world, with ocean friends.

Tales of the Swaying Palms

When palms start to break dance in the sun,
You can bet your flip-flops, the party's begun.
Coconuts fall like unexpected jazz,
Watch out below for these nutty chaps!

A seagull's serenade might cause a stir,
It squawks a tune, oh what a blur!
While crabs with their moves steal the show,
But not quite sure how to cha-cha slow.

The breeze whispers secrets through the leaves,
Playing hide and seek, can you believe?
Dancing shadows on the sandy floor,
Give me a drink, I might need more!

With laughter ringing like a bell's chime,
Every moment here is simply sublime.
So grab a chair, soak in the vibes,
In this wild land where joy thrives.

Journey through the Mangrove Heart

In mangroves where the mud crabs prance,
They have more rhythm than a dance-off chance.
With roots like noodles, they sway and bend,
You might spot a fish, hiding its friend.

The iguanas laugh, hanging on a branch,
Each one dressed for a comedy ranch.
Their sunbaked smiles can't be denied,
Who knew lizards had so much pride?

A hidden gator slips by with sass,
Thinking it's stealthy, but oh, what a pass!
With a splash and a roll, he's gone in a blink,
"Did you see that?!" you laugh till you stink.

A boat full of friends, we giggle and chime,
Lost in the mangroves, and we're just fine.
The tales we weave in this muddy embrace,
Turn every trip into a wild race.

Fragments of a Coastal Reverie

On the beach, where the sand likes to tickle,
A crab tells a joke, then dances a sickle.
Behind it, the waves are playing charades,
Each splash a punchline, in sun-soaked glades.

Seashells gossip as they lie in the sun,
"Did you hear the one about that dumb bun?"
Starfish laugh quietly, stuck to the floor,
But watch them closely—they wiggle for more!

A seagull photobombs my sandy sunbake,
"What's with your tan?" it caws, like a rake.
The sun dips lower, we're all in a spin,
With sand in our hair, we can't help but grin.

As nighttime descends with its glittery light,
We share our best jokes 'til the morning is bright.
In this realm of laughter, we've found our tune,
With giggles and guffaws beneath the moon.

Chronicles of the Serene Bay

In a bay where the boats wear silly caps,
They rock with the rhythm, and steer with a flap.
A pelican dives in, makes quite a scene,
Pulls up a mystery, a fish that's obscene!

The sun sparkles like a wink from a friend,
While dolphins leap high, no need to pretend.
"Catch me if you can!" they tease from the waves,
With splashes of joy, the beachgoer braves.

A beach ball escapes with a wild little bounce,
Rolling past sunbathers; oh, what a pounce!
With laughter erupting, we chase it down fast,
In this bay of silliness, we're free at last.

As dusk paints a canvas of pinks and blues,
We spin tales of fun while sipping the hues.
Such stories we share, each one a delight,
In the bay where giggles shatter the night.

Oasis of the Melodic Waves

In the hammock, I sway with delight,
Coconuts fall, giving quite a fright.
The seagulls squawk, they dance with glee,
Over my chips, they aim to spree.

Sandy toes and a sunburned nose,
Chasing crabs as the cool tide flows.
A fish tried to swim, but tripped on his fin,
Guess he won't be catching a meal or a grin!

Drinks with umbrellas, oh what a sight!
Juggling pineapples, my fruit-filled night.
Turtles roam while I sip my punch,
Who knew beach life could be this much fun?

Laughter dances like waves on the shore,
Life's too short—let's just roar!
With sandcastles that soon will collapse,
Today we live, with no time for naps!

Heartbeats of the Endless Beach

On the boardwalk, there's a fabulous crowd,
Ice cream cones melt, oh my, how loud!
Flip-flops slapping, everyone's a race,
Sunburns add color, just part of the chase.

Seagulls plotting to snatch my fries,
I stand like a guard, with creative lies.
"Those are stale!" I shout with pride,
As they circle back on their feathery glide.

A beach ball bounces, it's quite the scene,
A kid takes a dive, dresses all green.
Sand in my sandwich, what a surprise,
Every bite feels like a grainy disguise!

As evening falls and the stars light the sky,
We giggle at sailors who drunkly sigh.
Tomorrow's a lottery, come try your luck,
In this beachy haven, with all kinds of luck!

Whispers of the Sea Breeze

The sea breeze tickles like a cheeky cat,
Playing tag with my straw hat.
Splashes of water, a playful sneak,
That crab just waved, but what did he speak?

With jellyfish gliding in graceful parade,
I tried to dance, but I only delayed.
A dolphin snickered at my moves so bold,
Here's a mash-up of laughter, pure gold!

Sunset sherbet, a canvas divine,
Seagulls holding a comical wine.
With shells as earrings, we strut with flair,
Every grain of sand says, "Just don't care."

In waves of laughter, we ride the tide,
The ocean's secrets, a whimsical guide.
Let's toss our worries and catch some waves,
In this laughter-filled world, it's joy that saves!

Coral Dreams at Dusk

Under coral skies, dreams twist and twirl,
A starfish wears shades for a magical whirl.
The fish gossip in their gleaming parade,
While crabs play poker on a sunken jade.

With jellybeans bobbing in a coconut bowl,
We sip on fruit punch—a hilarious goal.
A mermaid giggles deep in her lair,
While seaweed dances, tossing its hair!

As evening spills over this canvas so bright,
Waves whisper jokes, under the moonlight.
A treasure map leads to laughter galore,
Where seashells chime, and the sea laughs more.

Now as the stars wink, it's time for a cheer,
For every good joke delivers a tear.
In this coral wonder where mischief reigns,
Laughter is the currency that never wanes!

Dance of the Shorebirds

Fluffy legs on sandy stage,
They prance and twirl, an avian rage.
With wind-blown feathers, they strike a pose,
Chasing each wave, dodging their toes.

A crab on its back, calls out in glee,
'You dance like a fool, come join me!'
They flap and they squawk, a comical sight,
Until the tide crashes, ending the night.

Faded Footprints on Bright Sands

Footprints trailing where fun once thrived,
Each step a story, all joy contrived.
But wait, what's this? A snail's slow race,
Spreading the laughter all over the place.

Caught in a swirl, a flip flop flies,
A dancer's delight, under the skies.
The tide rolls in, erasing the tales,
While seagulls conspire, plotting new wails.

A Palette of Coastal Whispers

Colors blend where the sea laughs loud,
A painting of joy, it draws a crowd.
A sunburnt tourist, bright as a flare,
Waves greet him with a salty stare.

Flip-flops squeak like a duck in distress,
As he tumbles over in a comical mess.
But up he pops, with a grin so wide,
As waves applaud his slapstick ride.

Harmonies of the Tidal Moon

Under a moon that winks with glee,
Crabs tap dance to the sound of the sea.
Starfish sway in rhythm divine,
While clams hum low, sipping their brine.

A dolphin jumps, it plays peek-a-boo,
Making the tourists yell, "What's that, whooo?"
Laughter rings out, a harmonious tune,
As nature's song plays, under the moon.

Swaying Palms in the Breeze

Under the sun, palms twist and twirl,
They dance to the rhythm, a leafy swirl.
With coconuts laughing, they tell a joke,
As beachgoers stumble, then all burst and poke.

A crab joins the party, with moves so neat,
He sidesteps along, to the catchy beat.
Flip-flops fly off as I dive to the sand,
The ocean just giggles, it's a wild band.

Seagulls squawk loudly, in comedic cheer,
They steal my sandwich, then disappear.
With drinks in our hands, the laughter flows,
We're all just goofs, that everyone knows.

Secrets of the Silken Shores

The shores whisper secrets, in soft, sandy tones,
Shells gossip like kids, with silly old moans.
I buried my treasures, but lost track of time,
Now I search for my sunglasses, oh aren't they sublime?

A flopping fish flirts and draws quite a crowd,
With winks and splashes, he's swimming so loud.
I try to recount all the laughs that I've had,
While seagulls snicker, at the sight of my plaid.

The tide takes my troubles, as waves roll away,
But they return silly, like a kid on a sway.
Sandcastles wobble, their turrets all lean,
I declare this beach a ridiculous scene!

The Language of Seashells

Seashells argue, in colors so bright,
One says, "I'm the best!" the other takes flight.
They gossip and bicker, their tales all absurd,
While I laugh aloud at their voice, like a bird.

In my bucket I gather these saucy old shells,
As they trade silly tales of their oceanic dwells.
I toss them a few words, in return they just bark,
New slang from the coast, it's quite the spark!

They teach me to giggle at waves rolling by,
And how to dance silly, under the sky.
Flavors of fun in the salt-kissed air,
The seashells and I form a goofy old pair.

Mists of Morning Over Calm Waters

Morning mist settles, all fluffy and white,
It swirls around legs, oh what a sight!
A pelican ponders, with a comical frown,
As he thinks of his breakfast, he's missing his crown.

I slip on a shell, go down with a splash,
The morning mist giggles, when my pants make a crash.
In a towel turban, I dance like a fool,
The ocean just chuckles, enjoying the rule.

The sun peeks out, the show gets more bright,
With laughter and fun, what a marvelous sight!
We all come together, like seaweed on sand,
In mists of the morning, let laughter expand!

Ephemeral Moments in Beachcomber's Bliss

A flip-flop flung into the air,
Lands on a crab without a care.
Sandcastles wobble, kids begin to scream,
As the tide pulls back, it's a crazy dream.

Seagulls squawk like they own the place,
Chasing after snacks at a lightning pace.
With sunscreen smeared across their nose,
Sunburned tourists strike a funny pose.

Buckets filled with shells and bits,
But mostly sand, oh what a hit!
The beach ball bounces, kids do cheer,
But watch your head when it's coming near!

As the sun dips down, it's time to snack,
Whipped cream pies that hit the back.
With laughter echoing in salty air,
What a moment, a joyful affair!

Ocean's Canvas of Shifting Colors

Look at the water, it's changing hues,
Can't tell if it's a prank or a ruse.
The waves are blue, then turn to green,
Is that a fish or just a bean?

A sunburned poet with paper and pen,
Trying to catch the colors again.
A pelican poses, oh what a sight,
With a fish in its beak and a beak full of bite!

With each crashing wave comes a gaggle of fun,
Lifeguard in shades, playing with a bun.
Beach umbrellas like mushrooms sprout,
Hiding chubby toes without a doubt.

At sundown, the sky's in a brawl,
Fighting orange, pink, and purple for all.
Just don't forget your drink in hand,
Or you might end up falling in sand!

Rendezvous at Sunset Bay

At sunset bay, things get quite silly,
As crabs dance like some night-time filly.
Flip a beach towel in a jolly twist,
And wave at the fish that you might have missed.

Swimmers splashing, kids giggle with glee,
Whispers of dolphins, come swim with me!
But wait, is that a mermaid I spy?
Or just a dog with a very wet tie?

The beach bonfire crackles with cheer,
While marshmallows fly—who knows where they land here?
Saltwater tales mix with giggles and yells,
As sand gets stuck in our sticky swells.

As stars pop out, the night goes amiss,
With friendship so sweet, nothing is amiss.
We'll laugh and we'll dance under starlit skies,
At sunset bay, fun never dies!

The Cadence of Rolling Waves

The ocean hums a silly tune,
As surfboards wobble like they're on a spoon.
The tide comes in with a cheeky grin,
Pulling back giggles from where they begin.

A dolphin does flips, trying to show off,
While a crab steals snacks from the beachside trough.
A surfcast fisherman tossing his line,
Reels in a shoe, oh what a find!

Sandcastles crumble, laughter erupts,
As a friendly seagull steals some lunch cups.
With every splash, the joys do grow,
And little ones squeal, "Hey there, let's go!"

With rolling waves come stories and fun,
Of bonfire kisses when day is done.
So dance with the tides, let your worries wave,
For life's a beach, just dig and behave!

Journey Through the Warm Waters

We set sail on a banana boat,
With piña coladas in hand,
The captain wore a silly hat,
That blew away on the sand.

Dolphins joined our singing quest,
They danced like they were high,
While seagulls tried to steal our snacks,
With a very cheeky eye.

Our boat spun round, we laughed aloud,
As the sun began to set,
A jellyfish waved, it's nice to meet!
When a wave caused a big regret!

As we splashed and tumbled through,
The water tickled our toes,
Every wave a giggle, my friend,
Who knew that fun could flow?

Cascading Rain and Sapphire Skies

Raindrops danced like tiny frogs,
On my sunburned nose,
Clouds dripped down their cotton fluff,
Where no one ever knows.

A pirate ship made of cookie dough,
Floated by on a breeze,
With first mates who wore sock puppets,
Strumming tunes with such ease.

Umbrellas turned into kites today,
Swept up with a gust of glee,
We laughed as we tumbled around,
In a wild game of spree!

Coconuts fell like bowling balls,
Crashing down on the grass,
We rolled and groaned in puddles bright,
And begged for time to pass!

Enchantment Along the Coastline

On a stroll by the sparkling shore,
We discovered seaweed wigs,
Worn by crabs in stylish hats,
And mermaids with silly digs.

Sandcastles with moats of soda pop,
Grew taller than my head,
While dolphins played peek-a-boo,
'Round every beach umbrella spread.

Turtles raced their tiny toes,
In a most absurd competition,
While we cheered with guffaws and glee,
Landing quite the strange position!

The sun set low on the horizon's line,
With giggles echoing still,
Each wave whispered secrets to the moon,
And stamped our hearts with thrill!

Threads of Seafoam and Sunlight

A thread of sun wrapped 'round my head,
Like a noodle in a bowl,
I twirled as the sea sang sweetly,
Making joy my only goal.

The seafoam tickled at my feet,
As crabs got mad and scuttled,
They waved their claws as if to say,
'Hey human, quit the puddle!'

The sand was warm like grandma's hug,
As I tried to stand and sway,
Then boom! I tripped, and up I flew,
But landed only by the bay.

A conch shell played a trumpet tune,
Out came fish in a choreo,
We joined the dance, all smiles abound,
In a beachside show, a free-for-all!

A Canvas of Lush Green and Blue

The palm trees dance with glee,
While I trip on a flip-flop spree.
A parrot squawks a joke or two,
I laugh so hard, I lose my shoe.

Bright flowers peek and start to sway,
As I try to find my way.
A squirrel steals my snack so quick,
His little face? A comic flick.

Beneath a sun that's shining bright,
My sunscreen's on; oh what a sight!
I slip and slide upon the sand,
Geckos giggle—oh, isn't life grand?

So here I float in azure bliss,
With nature's humor, hard to miss.
Laughter rises with each tide,
In this wild world, I take a ride.

Conversations with the Sea Shells

I asked a shell about its day,
It just looked back and said, 'No way!'
A starfish chimed in with a grin,
'Life's a beach; let's dive right in!'

A crab nearby, with tiny speech,
Said, 'Watch out! Don't get too close to me, each!
I've claws, you know; I used them once,
To fend off seagulls, oh those dunce!'

The tide comes in; the shells all cheer,
But loud waves have the crabs in fear.
'Quick! Hide!' they shout in frantic fun,
While I just laugh, soaking in sun.

They share their tales of shore adventures,
Of fishy friends and distant ventures.
With each odd story, I can tell,
These shells surely know how to dwell!

Sunsets that Paint the Horizon

As daylight fades, I grab my drink,
The clouds all blush; what do they think?
A flamingo poses, strikes a pose,
With colors splashed, it surely glows.

I watch the sky, it paints with flair,
A golden twist beyond compare.
And then a breeze? Oh what a troll,
It steals my hat; it must be whole.

Laughter echoes as the ship sails past,
'Is that a boat or a giant mast?'
With silly thoughts, my mind takes flight,
As twinkling stars begin the night.

So here I stand with joy and mirth,
Embracing each moment of this earth.
With every sunset, laughs unfold,
In colors bright, life's stories told.

Embrace of the Island Breeze

The breeze arrives with playful shouts,
It tips my drink, then dances about.
A coconut rolls, that's not so sweet,
'Another round?' it taunts my feet.

Sandcastles rise, but waves don't care,
They crash with glee; it's quite a scare.
The crabs complain, 'We can't hold still!'
While seagulls play the ultimate thrill.

'Join me, friend!' the ocean calls,
'Let's ride the waves and break down walls!'
But just as I dive, I get a shock,
The water's cold; surprise! No clock.

Yet still we laugh, this wild affair,
As winds blow whispers through my hair.
In this embrace, oh what a tease,
I find my joy in every breeze.

Reflections of a Distant Dawn

Morning light begins to tease,
Awakens the chatter of sleepy bees.
A crow steals my breakfast toast,
While I ponder which critter's my ghost.

The coconut sways, it teeters and tilts,
So many fruits with unknown guilt.
The sun is a prankster, wild and bold,
Laughing at secrets the dawn has told.

Crabs in suits of armor parade,
They dance on the sand like a grand charade.
Seagulls squawk their morning report,
As I sit here, stuck in my fort.

But on this shore, bright dreams align,
Where ocean waves sip the fruit of the vine.
Laughter rolls like a wave on the bay,
In this silly dawn, I lose my way.

Currents of Color in the Coral Reef

Fish in tuxedos dart and glide,
In a sugar rush, they swim with pride.
A clownfish jests, a true witty genius,
Makes even the seaweed feel so Venus.

Bubble-blowing pufferfish puff,
Turning tiny tots to blushing fluff.
Shrimp in shades of neon lights,
Their disco moves are out of sight.

The anemone swings like a silly old friend,
Waiting for seafood surprises around the bend.
With colors so bright, a real fashion spree,
The sea is the runway, come dance with me!

But beware of the grouper with an attitude,
He'll laugh at your jokes, then change the mood.
Beneath the waves, antics unfold,
Where every coral holds a story retold.

Sunlit Pathways Through the Jungle

In the jungle, where giggles reside,
Vines gossip while critters collide.
Monkeys swing from tree to tree,
Claiming the crown as king of the spree.

Parrots squawk in a vivid parade,
Their vibrant feathers are surely handmade.
A turtle insists he's speedy like light,
But takes a nap instead, what a sight!

Lizards in shades that sparkle and shine,
Stare down the toucan, sipping on brine.
Each step reveals a riddle to crack,
Where vines might tickle, and laughter comes back.

But watch out for bugs with comedic flair,
They buzz with a beat that's hard to bear.
In this sunlit maze where wonders convene,
Life is a jest, and we're part of the scene!

The Rhythm of Pacific Dreams

Waves roll in with a slap and a splash,
Dancing foam like a jolly bash.
A dolphin spins, mimicking my grin,
In this ocean party, let laughter begin.

Surfboards wobble like jellies on sand,
As each ride is met with a twist or a hand.
Seashells giggle beneath the bright sun,
They share old tales of sea monsters fun!

Sunsets melt like ice cream treats,
While I try balancing on wobbly seats.
The rhythm of waves sings a jig,
It pulls my heart with a dance so big.

So grab a friend and catch the tide,
Let the ocean's humor be your guide.
In this joyous sea, all worries elope,
With laughter and rhythm, we find our hope.

Resilient Roots of the Mangrove

In muddy waters they swell and sway,
Holding tight where the crabs play.
With dance moves that make fish laugh,
And a game of tag with a cheeky calf.

They poke fun at the waves that crash,
Waving roots that seem to splash.
Paddling in mud like a champ,
These roots deserve a victory stamp!

With every gust, they giggle and twist,
In nature's dance, they can't resist.
Their party vibe causes quite a stir,
As otters come for a wiggly slur.

So when you stroll by this leafy jive,
Remember the roots that come alive.
In every splash, there's joy to find,
In laughter's rhythm, they're perfectly aligned.

In the Shadow of Leaning Palms

Under the palms that lean just right,
Lizards play tag, what a funny sight!
With a wink and a sway, they dodge a shoe,
While seagulls squawk songs that are way too blue.

A gust of wind makes the branches dance,
As coconuts fall in a clumsy prance.
The shadows flicker like a silly show,
Where every leaf has a rhyme to throw.

In the golden sun, they take a rest,
Competing for who's the funniest guest.
Stories exchanged in a breeze so bright,
With old tales told 'til the fall of night.

So if you lay beneath their sway,
You'll hear their giggles float your way.
In the tranquil space of their leafy throne,
Laughter rings out, you're never alone.

Soft Footprints at Water's Edge

Along the shore where the soft sands lie,
Footprints wander beneath the sky.
A crab with swagger steals the scene,
While a dog thinks he's the king, so keen!

With each splash, laughter fills the air,
A flip-flop's saga is quite the affair.
A plop, a splash, then a slippery chase,
As seagulls squawk in a wacky race.

The tide rolls up with a cheeky grin,
Washing away the tales within.
But don't be fooled, they return on cue,
With new sandy jokes, just for you.

So stamp your feet and enjoy the play,
At the water's edge, fun is on display.
With giggles and splashes, the day flies by,
In a dance of footprints beneath the sky.

The Call of the Salty Winds

When salty breezes start to call,
The kites go up and it's a ball!
Flip-flops screech as children race,
While the ocean laughs at their wild pace.

Winds whip through coconut trees so high,
Carrying whispers and a friendly sigh.
They tease the waves to come and play,
In a constant dance of cheeky display.

Seagulls crack jokes from their windy perch,
Leading everyone in a sunshine search.
But watch your hat, don't let it fly,
Because in the wind, it could wave goodbye!

So heed the call when the breezes sing,
To laugh and play, oh what joy they bring.
With every gust, let humor flow,
In a festival of winds, go with the flow!

A Palette of Island Reveries

With sunburned noses, we chase the breeze,
Flip-flops flying, laughing with ease.
A parrot steals my fruity drink,
While I ponder how much I can think.

The waves crash softly, like giggles galore,
As crabs in the sand plot a dance on the shore.
My towel's a blanket, my drink's in a cup,
Yet here I am, wondering how to get up.

Seagulls squawk out their funny old tales,
While fish wear sunglasses, swimming in scales.
A beach ball bounces like laughter in flight,
Sandy snacks hidden from seagulls' delight.

In daisy chains woven from vibrant blooms,
We twirl through the island, dodging the zooms.
Life's an adventure with giggles and grins,
At sunset we toast with our fruity swim bins.

Conversations with the Drifting Clouds

Clouds whisper secrets in cottony fluff,
I ask them sweetly, 'Is life ever tough?'
They giggle in puffs, drifting by with delight,
While I wiggle my toes in the warm, salty light.

One cloud claims power to paint with the sun,
While another tosses rain just for fun.
They bet on the sky, who's winning tonight,
With thunderous laughter that's quite a delight.

A fluffy brigade in their white, lofty land,
They invent silly games while I make a stand.
I challenge them kindly to a race with the sea,
But they just float higher, laughing so free.

With jellyfish politics and dolphin debates,
They gossip and giggle about fish of all fates.
I have my own stories, oh don't you agree?
As foam on the waves waves back up at me!

Murmurs of Ancient Tides

Old shells spin tales of their salty yore,
Each grain of sand knows what's washed ashore.
I sit on the beach with a puzzled look,
While crabs exchange whispers, like pages in a book.

The seaweed sings songs of the deep, hidden realms,
Where fish trade their bargain on glittery gems.
A starfish plays chess with a seashell so grand,
While a seagull squawks loudly, 'I rule this fine land!'

As the salty breeze dances through my hair,
I chuckle at dolphins that leap in midair.
They wink at me slyly, making quite a splash,
As I trip over coolers—it's quite a nice crash!

Old hooks and old nets weave a history's tale,
In every wave's murmur, a secret to unveil.
While the ocean chuckles, forever so bright,
I dip my toes softly, and feel just right.

Where the Sky Meets the Emerald Sea

The sky drops confetti, squishy and blue,
As I snorkel for treasure—a crusty old shoe!
The fish giggle softly, they know I'm a clown,
Waving their fins, as I nearly fall down.

But wait! What's that? A coconut flies!
I duck as it zooms past me—a surprise!
The sunbeams are plotting some shenanigans now,
While I juggle my snacks, looking puzzled, somehow!

With laughter from boats swaying tenderly near,
I dance with the tide, oblivious to fear.
The waves toss me gently, a game we all play,
As flippers and snorkels join in on the fray.

A beach bonfire crackles under the stars,
We share funny stories, and joke about scars.
As the sky blends with ocean, the world feels so free,
Where mirth and amusement are always the key!

Kaleidoscope of Oceanic Skies

Seagulls squawk a silly song,
While starfish dance the night along.
A crab wears shades, oh what a sight,
Waving at waves and feeling bright.

Jellyfish float with jelly minds,
Their bobbing way, so unrefined.
The dolphins giggle, flipping high,
Laughing with fish, oh me, oh my!

Waves play tag upon the shore,
Each splash a chuckle, wanting more.
The sandcastles wobble, tip and lean,
As if they're laughing, oh so keen.

A sunburnt lobster, red and bold,
Rides the tide in stories told.
With winks and grins, the ocean hums,
In this wild world, joy always comes.

Crashing Emotions and Salty Sprays

Seashells gossip, sharing tales,
Of coral reefs and sunny gales.
Octopus pranks with eight sly hands,
While dolphins flip at our commands.

The shore's a circus, waves the show,
Where beach balls bounce, and kids run low.
Laughter echoes, but watch your hat,
A sneaky tide says, 'Just like that!'

Frisbees fly like silly birds,
In this play place, without words.
Time wobbles like a jelly's jig,
While hermit crabs dance a little dig.

The piña coladas, sweet and bright,
Mix joy and laughter, day and night.
With salty air and smiles galore,
Who would ever want to leave this shore?

The Lure of Hidden Coves

In secret nooks where crabs convene,
A treasure map is drawn, unseen.
Where coconuts giggle on the ground,
And scatter the shades of joy around.

Mermaids whisper with a splash,
The sea's a stage, like a madcap bash.
Fish in bow ties swim in style,
Throwing seaweed confetti with a smile.

The turtles slow dance, moving wise,
Under a sun that shines and pries.
Shells vibrating with laughter, what a spree,
In hidden coves where we're all carefree!

Uncles in floaties look so grand,
As they paddle their boats of sand.
With a flip-flop here and a beach ball there,
Fun is brewing everywhere!

Bright Breezes and Dappled Light

A parasol tilted, caught in flight,
Ducks swim by, oh what a sight!
Chasing shadows on the sand,
   Silly seagulls take a stand.

The surfboards race on bubbly waves,
Each paddle splash, a giggle saves.
Moments flutter in the sun's warm glow,
With friend-filled laughter, watch it grow.

Umbrellas wobble, drinks go 'clink!'
As sippin' pirates make us think.
Funky sun hats, bold and wide,
Catch the breeze, like a wild ride.

A treasure hunt for shells galore,
What can be better than this outdoor lore?
In dappled light and fun-filled dreams,
Life shimmers bright, bursting at the seams!

Flavors of Island Spice

Pineapple salsa on my plate,
With a taste that makes me celebrate.
Coconut laughter fills the air,
As mangoes dance without a care.

The curry's hot, my tongue's on fire,
But I can't resist, I must retire.
Plantains sing a happy tune,
While I juggle fruit in the afternoon.

Jerk chicken winks on the grill,
Telling me I've had my fill.
But oh, that piña colada's dream,
Makes me sway and laugh and scream!

Sugarcane whispers in the breeze,
Tickling my nose with such sweet ease.
And with each bite, I can't help but chuckle,
Life's a feast, in this spice-laden puddle!

The Embrace of a Gentle Wave

A wave approached, all fluffy and bright,
It swirled and twirled with pure delight.
I waved back, but oh, what a splash,
Soaked my sunscreen in quite the crash.

The tide tickles toes, laughs on the shore,
I slip and flip, then belly flop more.
A seagull giggles at my surprise,
Calling me silly with rolling eyes.

Floating like a fish, I try to sway,
But those waves have jokes at my display.
They pull me back, then let me go,
I wave farewell, but return for the show!

In this watery dance, I find my bliss,
Life is a jest, no moment I'll miss.
So, here's to laughter, in sunlit foam,
With every splash, this will always be home!

Driftwood Stories Unfolding

A piece of driftwood tells a tale,
Of ocean journeys and winds that sail.
Each knot and twist, a laugh it hides,
Adventures of fish where humor abides.

It saw a crab in a dance-off so bold,
With moves so silly, I'm told it was gold.
And a dolphin, who did a double backflip,
While wearing a hat—the crowd took a sip!

As the sun set low, the wood seemed to grin,
Recalling the laughter, where all had been in.
The sand whispered secrets to the moonlit shore,
While driftwood chuckled—who could ask for more?

So gather 'round, for stories so grand,
Of silly sea creatures, all together they stand.
With every wave that kisses the sand,
A driftwood comedy, isn't life simply planned?

A Reverie of Waves and Stars

Under the stars, waves start to giggle,
Spilling their secrets with a playful wiggle.
Each foam-filled bubble seems to say,
Let's dance all night, come what may!

I lie on the sand, lost in a dream,
As the ocean hums a whimsical theme.
A starfish croons, a barrel of laughs,
While crabs do the cha-cha with stylized gaffs.

The sky's a canvas, painted so bright,
While the waves play tag with the moon's silver light.
I chuckle at fish, in their underwater play,
Sliding like dancers, with no care in their sway.

As dawn approaches, the giggles still swell,
With waves and stars, all under love's spell.
So let's raise a toast to this whimsy so free,
In a world of our laughter, for you and for me!

Starlit Paths Across the Sea

Beneath the stars, we dance and prance,
With flip-flops squeaking, we take a chance.
A crab in shades joins our lively cheer,
While seagulls squawk, we down our beer.

Waves keep rolling, a secret trip,
A fish on surfboard says, "Take a dip!"
We splash and giggle, the moon's our guide,
Oh, to be silly, in our ocean stride.

In the distance, a dolphin grins wide,
Says, "Why walk when you can glide?"
With laughter echoing through the night,
We bid farewell to the soft moonlight.

But wait! Is that a seaweed hat?
Fashion faux pas? Imagine that!
Yet here we are, in blissful fun,
Riding the waves, the night's just begun.

Coral Caves and Sunlit Rides

In a coral cave, we play hide and seek,
My friend wore goggles, but just couldn't peek.
A parrotfish laughs, points its fin,
"You're not a dolphin—just a swimwin!"

Sunlit rides on a banana boat,
Someone yells, "Hold on!" while we float.
Then we spin, flip, in a splashy spree,
A mermaid shouts, "Swim like a bee!"

Sandy toes and glittering smiles,
Each wave catches us, we're in for miles.
The sun's a spotlight, oh what a scene,
Where even the seaweed is fashion-renowned green.

As we tumble back, hearts light and carefree,
Our giggles echo, "You're stuck with me!"
With coral and sun, we've made our claim,
In a day of laughter, a silly game.

Reflections in a Tidepool

Peering close at a tidepool scene,
A tiny shrimp looks like it's been on caffeine.
It wriggles and giggles, what a funny sight,
Taking selfies under the sun's bright light.

Next door, a clam's throwing a smackdown,
With purple shells that could win a crown.
"Oh come on, friend, let's have a race!"
The seaweed shakes, keeping up the pace.

Starfish lounge as if on a beach,
Filet of mermaid, just out of reach.
Clams cover their shells, grumbling loud,
"Why must we put up with this crowd?"

But laughter fills every bubbly bob,
While crabs play drums in an old eel's mob.
In this tidepool giggle fest we find,
Nature's best laugh, all intertwined.

The Allure of Island Lanterns

Island lanterns flicker, what a sight,
Making us dance until the morning light.
A coconut falls, knocks my friend down,
We laugh so hard, we could coat the town.

Jellyfish waltz, in ball gowns they glow,
While sea cucumbers put on a show.
"Here comes the conch!" it dares to croon,
Yet slips on a shell, "Not my best tune!"

It's a merry-go-round, a raucous cheer,
As fish offer drinks saying "Come on, dear!"
With a wink and a flip, they swirl around,
"What's next? A fish dance, how profound!"

As lanterns sway in the gentle air,
We're lost in laughter, nothing to compare.
With stars as our buddies, the night won't end,
Here's to island nights—and the fun they send!

www.ingramcontent.com/pod-product-compliance
Lightning Source LLC
Chambersburg PA
CBHW070318120526
44590CB00017B/2727